Let the Life Flow

A BOOK BY PRIYANKA MADAAN

BLUEROSE PUBLISHERS
India | U.K.

Copyright © Priyanka Madaan 2025

All rights reserved by author. No part of this publication may be reproduced, stored in a retrieval system or transmitted in any form or by any means, electronic, mechanical, photocopying, recording or otherwise, without the prior permission of the author. Although every precaution has been taken to verify the accuracy of the information contained herein, the publisher assumes no responsibility for any errors or omissions. No liability is assumed for damages that may result from the use of information contained within.

BlueRose Publishers takes no responsibility for any damages, losses, or liabilities that may arise from the use or misuse of the information, products, or services provided in this publication.

For permissions requests or inquiries regarding this publication, please contact:

BLUEROSE PUBLISHERS
www.BlueRoseONE.com
info@bluerosepublishers.com
+91 8882 898 898
+4407342408967

ISBN: 978-93-6783-170-0

Cover Design: Aman Sharma
Typesetting: Pooja Sharma

First Edition: February 2025

ACKNOWLEDGEMENT

This book, while being a collection of words, is a part of my heart molded by love, support, and lessons that came with the amazing people in my life. While I sit down to pen these acknowledgements, I feel a sense of huge gratitude toward each and every person who has been a part of my journey so far.

To me lovely parents, you are my first home, my safe haven and the very roots that anchor me. Thank you for the unconditional love, endless patience, and sacrifices. If I learned anything about the virtues of kindness, resilience, and humility, it was all thanks to you. I want you to know that everything that I am today and everything I aspire to become is all because of you.

To my partners-in-crime, my siblings, you guys were my very first friends, my accomplices in crime, and lifetime companions. Thanks for being there for me & always having my back through all the triumphs and woes. From the times filled with belly-aching laughter that made me forget my worries even if for a short while, to the occasional disagreements have all helped to make so many moments special in my life. Thank you for all the cheering that you have been doing for me and for keeping my secrets confidential.

Special mention to my husband who is my biggest supporter, and my best friend, thanks for believing in me at times when even I had lost faith in myself. I don't even have words to describe how grateful I am for your love, patience, and quiet strength that has been my foundation. You have seen me at my best and my worst, yet you stood by me through it all. Thank you for being 'you'.

To my children, I hope you know you hold my heart in the palm of your hands. You have actually taught me stuff about life I never thought was possible—about how my heart can store endless love, being resilient, seeing the world through 'innocent' colored glasses. Thanks for reminding me how beautiful life can be and why I should keep striving to become a better version of myself everyday.

Thank you to my in-laws for welcoming me so lovingly and accepting me into your lives with open arms. It is through your warmth and kindness that I have always, and continue to, feel at home. I really treasure the bond we share and the memories we have created together.

Thanks to my ride or die, my friends, thank you for being the best chosen family I could ever have. You all, each in your unique ways, contributed something special in my life. Whether through an honest, open conversation or a shared laugh or just by your quiet presence, each one of you has brought your own meaning into my life. Your belief in me has always been the greatest motivation for me.

And lastly, I thank each and every person who has ever crossed my path. It doesn't matter if you were in my life for just a moment or if you are here to stay. Every single moment with you all has made me grow. You have all made a mark in my heart, and you've helped shape me into the person I am today.

It is because of this love, support, and encouragement that I have received from all of you that this book exists. This book is a piece of my journey; I hope it reflects the gratitude and love that every single one of you inspires within me.

Thank you from the depths of my heart. I love you all.

Love,

Priyanka Madaan

PREFACE

There are days when it feels like the world is moving a little too fast, isn't it? So, during those times what I do is just, you know, exist. Even if the world is already miles and miles away from me, I just stroll. And I think those moments prove to me just how human it is to slow down, walk, and maybe even take a rest. When other people's pace is a little too fast for you, just create your own.

I have spent countless moments sitting serenely, watching the world around me rush by, and thinking why everyone is in a hurry. We all are so intent on winning, on reaching the next objective, that we forgot the beauty of simply living. We have made it into an unending marathon forgetting that life is long so it is okay to take it slow sometimes.

Which is why, these days, I have been going through books slowly, taking walks in the park, meditating, even investing in different hobbies. And it made me think whether living each day as it comes might be the kind of life that I'd like to have. Living in the present. Not wondering about yesterday, not thinking of tomorrow, just enjoying the little joys of today. To be alive is a gift and a blessing from God. Dwelling in life with zest and celebrating every victory and failure, it forms a way of giving thanks to God and the universe for its provisions.

This book is to help you shift from a victim mentality to that of a creator bringing along a deeper understanding of life's purposes. It's about allowing yourself to embrace life as it comes, to live in the little everyday moments. Because it's in the quiet, the in-between, where life feels the most real. This book is going to hold your hand and maneuver you to a life that feels like folding the laundry whose smell mimics that of the sunshine. A life that feels like finally eating home cooked meals after months or making notes in your favorite book with wobbly lines and crooked handwriting. A life that is gentle and kind. And once you reach the end of the book, you will realize that all you ever wanted was for life to feel like life—something you'd only be able to have once.

I remember reading somewhere that life isn't about how much we accomplish or how quickly we reach the top—it's about being present. Living each and every moment as it is. And I understand how hard that can be when the world demands speed, we borrow dreams from others like a debt, we learn that we need to become great only then we're worthy of life and in the process, life becomes a burden. But what if being left behind is a gift? How about catching up with ourselves in-between before resuming the race?

This book is for anyone who feels worn out by the rush of life, for those who long for a moment of peace. Let this be a gentle reminder that it's okay to slow down, to move at your own pace, and to simply breathe. Life, like water, flows in its own time. It shifts, it moves, and we can't always control it, but we can choose to go with the flow.

So as you read, I hope you'll find moments of reflection, of stillness. I hope this book reminds you that you don't have to race through life. That you can walk when others are sprinting. And that sometimes, slowing down is exactly what you need.

Because life isn't a race, and you are not behind. *Let life flow.*

CONTENTS

CHAPTER 1 (INTRODUCTION/LET LIFE FLOW) 1

CHAPTER 2 (SHARING IS CARING) 11

CHAPTER 3 (JUDGEMENT AND CRITICISM) 21

CHAPTER 4 (POWER OF ACCEPTANCE) 35

CHAPTER 5 (FORGIVENESS) 49

CHAPTER 6 (THE POWER OF INTENTION) 61

CHAPTER 7 (INTUITION) 75

CHAPTER 8 (THE POWER OF SILENCE) 89

CHAPTER 9 (THE POWER OF MANIFESTATION) 105

CHAPTER 10 (THE ART OF GRATITUDE) 119

AUTHOR'S NOTE 128

ABOUT THE BOOK 132

GRATITUDE JOURNAL 135

CHAPTER 1

(INTRODUCTION/LET LIFE FLOW)

In endless curves, the road continued forward, a ribbon of possibility winding through the Ladakh landscape's stark majestic beauty. Our car rose steadily, the air going thinner as we climbed higher, the hum of its engine harmonizing with the rhythm of my stream-of-thoughts. Outside the window the world looked like a rolling painting into motion, as if asleep, hillsides curled up like resting giants, shrouded in light, and black shadow, darkened at intervals by patches of green from which life tenuously clung.

It was nothing like the sort of beauty I was used to growing up amidst the coziness of Himachal Pradesh, where the emerald valleys embrace snow-white peaks time and again. Ladakh was different—minimalistic, raw, and powerful. Here, the earth breathed its primeval rhythm, untouched by human hands, untarnished by time. When the car took a sharp turn, the valley opened, and a stream flowed in a meandering path. The dark waters gleamed under the sun, carving a path with quiet determination.

Each hill seemed to have a story to tell. Some jagged and rugged, others sloping gently as in a bow to the sky. The colors changed with the light, painting an ever-changing masterpiece. I had only seen these pictures on the internet previously, but nothing could represent the surreal beauty that presented itself before my eyes, streams of dark water coursing through valleys, so hypnotic with their own movement. I found myself looking, unable to tear my gaze away. There was this rhythm in the flowing water itself, its quiet persistence which reaches deep inside. At that moment, one thing came into my head; *Life is just like this water. Always moving, always flowing.*

This realization came to me so clearly that I could hardly keep myself from shouting it out loud. I turned to my husband and exclaimed, "*Let life flow!*" He looked at me, smiled, and was a little puzzled. "*Okay…?*" he replied, unsure where I was going with that. "*No, no,*" I said, chuckling at his look of confusion. "*That is the name of my book!*" I could see him fight to hide a smile, but I didn't mind. The seed was planted. It suddenly dawned on me what the concept would be about. I longed to pen a self-help book which would remind people to live by life's flux, stopping for moments where one isn't merely breezing through days but simply living through them.

And in that car, I sat and thought about my life, how every twist and turn had led me to this place. Life is not about fighting the currents but learning to swim gracefully with them. We waste so much time opposing change, dreading the unfamiliar, that we forget how to be. However, as is with water passing through the valleys, life tends to make its way. It does not stop for barricades; it flows alongside them, over them or even through them if there is a necessity.

Throughout the drive towards Nubra Valley, I found myself thinking of the major events in my life, how much distance I have crossed, what hurdles I crossed, and what life taught me. Among all, one thing, however, stood out-the moment when my life had been irreversibly altered.

It was 9 February 1992. I remember being in twelfth standard at that time. I was sitting in Accounts class and sipping water from a bottle. Everything that day had been normal and usual till it wasn't. Without warning, a strange heaviness settled into my chest, and I felt my hands shaking while trying to steady the bottle. The room started spinning, and the bottle slipped from my hands before I knew what was happening. Darkness wrapped around me like a cloak.

When I woke up, I found myself lying in a hospital room that was lit a little too bright for my liking. My parents sat holding hands, with pale faces filled with worry. My friends stood near the door, unsure what to say. The doctor's voice was soft but firm as he told me the diagnosis: bronchitis asthma. I had no idea what it meant at that moment, but during the following months, things became clear.

The asthma attacks would come very frequently and unexpectedly, so my once carefree life became all about going to and fro from the hospitals and home, recovering. I was also highly sensitive to all that happened around me, dust, pollen, even very strong emotions would trigger an episode. It was like my body was a fragile shell and I was hating that feeling of vulnerability. All I wanted was to lead a normal life doing things people my age do instead of doing hospital reruns.

However, there was always light in even the darkest moments. My friends were around me with their laughter and support. Love from family was what held me together. It continued to push me as I slowly started adjusting to this new reality of life. Despite everything, the illness gave me strength. I realized that I could withstand so much more than I ever thought possible.

Even with all the tribulations, I finished the college course, earning a Diploma in Marketing and Public Relations. By the time I reached my early twenties, I was busy running conferences for the Ministry of External Affairs-a job which needed me to be confident and poised. It was then that I met my husband.

It was as if I found a missing part of me I didn't know was missing when I fell in love with him. He saw me for who I was; he accepted me with all my baggage, asthma and problems all. He is the quiet, steady presence grounding me even through the most turbulent times of my life. Marriage brought its own adventures. My husband encouraged me to prioritize the family, but he left me with the freedom to pursue my passions. Support from him gave me space to discover new avenues and homeopathy was one among them. I was inspired by my father-in-law who is a homeopathic doctor. This encouraged me to research alternative medicine. Balancing studies with bringing up two boys was not easy, but it was incredibly fulfilling. Slowly but surely, things started getting better in my health.

The journey towards healing was not linear. It included setbacks and occasional doubts, but I never faltered. Pranayama was a daily institution, and gradually the instances of asthma attacks began dwindling. This meant I hadn't used an inhaler for years by the time I took that journey to Nubra Valley. It felt like a win, not just over my asthma but over the disability I once thought defined me and made me who I am. But as I sat in the car, watching the water flow, I realized just how far I have come.

It had taken me 30 years and 7 months to be able to proclaim myself free of asthma. This was victory enough, not just to have no more illness but also to represent the journey taken. And now here I am, having survived all the twists and turns life had led me on and still standing firm. And now, finally ready to tell my story so that others may embrace their flow of life.

In that moment, standing on the cliff of Nubra Valley, I let out the breath I did not know I was holding and silently promised to myself that I would be writing this book, not merely for others, but for me, a celebration of resilience and love and the beauty of letting go.

And as the sun fell below the horizon, painting it in hues of orange and pink all over the sky, I found a deep sense of contentment and peace like never before inside me. The route ahead was uncertain, yet I knew that I was as ready to face it as that tiny stream moving through that valley which I have been describing.

So turning my smiling self toward my husband, I whispered, "*Let life flow*". I said it again but this time with a low and quiet conviction. He looked at me and smiled as well. We watched that stream disappear into the horizon, a reminder that the flow continues no matter where life may take us.

YOUR THOUGHTS

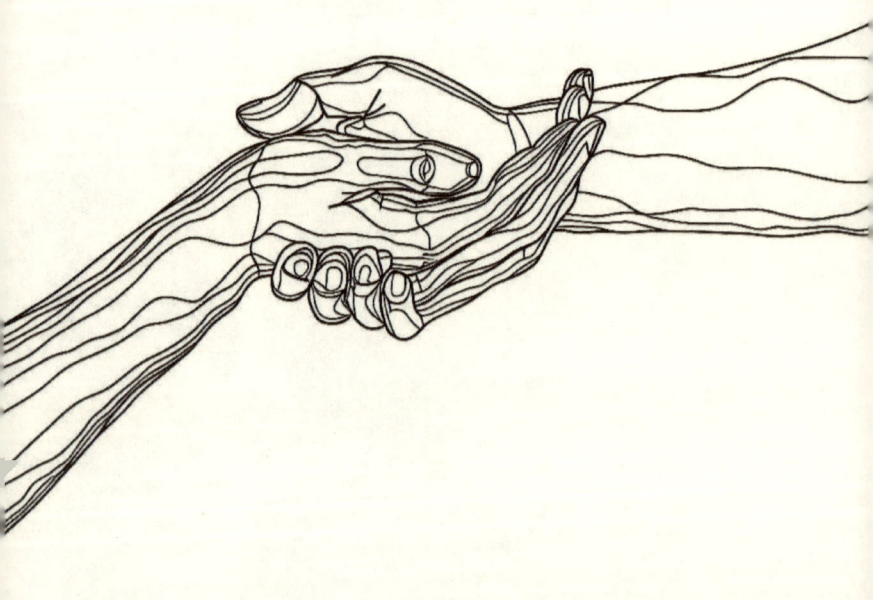

CHAPTER 2

(SHARING IS CARING)

Sharing has always been so instinctive for me, not only with tangible possessions but opening myself up as well so my experiences will be able to serve as a crossing to help someone get through some of their obstacles. To me, every story carries meaning; lessons learned, inspiration sparked, and realization that nudges someone a little bit closer to finding their truth. Looking back, I realised my story is just a stream of dots; every line of it seemed separate up until I stepped back a bit and noticed how well they all connected toward one big picture. Every incident that has affected my life has its uniqueness.

I came to find that the experiences we receive often come through our minds, karmic conditions, or even resistances we go through. Of course, thoughts are quite strong weapons. It took me even years to learn that actual reality is indeed a mirrored reflection of our thought-provoking expressions and our emotions. If I believed the world was made of untrustworthy people, then that's exactly what I'd attract. Our vibrations are like a magnet that pulls in experiences that match what we are putting out there. This isn't theoretical but it's a universal law, just like gravity, and just how gravity works day and night, so does this law.

But thoughts comprise only half of the picture. There is also karma—the invisible baggage which we carry with ourselves, lifetime after lifetime. Every time we are born, we are assigned the task of balancing a part of this karmic weight. It's like the universe hands you your assignment, and you're given the choice of looking at it or letting it hang. Rejection factors in, too. When people deny something – an idea, truth, or a situation, it often persists and is found again and again until a final confrontation is made with the force against which one is battling.

For years I thought "*letting life flow*" was to sit back and wait for something to happen. Yet, life taught me it is something completely different. To let life flow is to absorb it completely-the highs and the lows, moments of joy and days of despair. We do not question when happiness comes. We just rejoice. So why are we fighting against the dark days? Why resist them? They, too, form a part of the rhythm of life. The mantra that keeps going through my mind during those times is "*This too shall pass*." Nothing remains; neither the good, nor the bad. And though accepting all this is necessary, that does not mean we must sit idly. After all, life does require action. Problems are solved, possibilities are probed, and a better tomorrow achieved all in faith that the universe moves on its own beat.

If I look back today, I realize how I have come to this very understanding, which has shaped my life. As a child, everybody used to come to me, confide in me when they were troubled, advise me, and rely upon me. At that time, I didn't realize, but it was building within me this role of the "agony aunt" leading me into becoming a future life coach. But life took a detour from there. Marriage, child rearing, and family became my priorities, and my attention was focused on raising good humans. I wanted to shelter them, provide them with a safe haven. I even took it to the point of insistence on personally handling their transport to and from school and classes for tuition, not trusting the task to anyone else. To me, this was a method of keeping them out of harm's way while maximising time spent with the children. Those times were precious, filled with memorable moments of bedtime stories, and laughter, and watching them grow.

As I grew older, they no longer required me as much, and I found myself with empty time on my hands. At first, it seemed so hauntingly empty at times because I had put my career on hold for so long that I didn't even know where to start again. What I didn't then realize was that the universe had its own plan; and when it thought the moment was right, the push came.

Becoming a life coach wasn't sudden. It took years. And the foundation of getting here was first healing oneself. I struggled with severe asthma for a long period in my life—a thing, as it turns out now, pretty much completely rooted in my emotion. It happened when I was in class 11; we were shifting from Bhatinda to Noida. Soon after that, I also lost my grandmother whom I shared a very close relationship with. Her death left me severely lonely, and my subliminal mind captured this. Since then, all I could think was "I am alone."

Everyone was pointing their finger at the thermal power plant in Bhatinda as the reason for my asthma at that time. However, the actual culprit was much deeper; my body was reacting to my deeply buried unresolved emotions, my grief, and my constant fear of abandonment. I did not begin to heal until I started working on myself—examining my subconscious and letting those stuck emotions go.

It wasn't easy; it took peeling away layers of beliefs and stories that I carried for many years. It made me cry, rage, and reflect on all that needed to change. Every victory was like a small war won but still showed the mountain I needed to climb. Emotions, if not processed, do not go away. They find residence in the body and lead to diseases. A manifestation of such stuckness was my asthma - a signal that the body needed something to shift.

As I went further into this inner journey, I started seeing how much of my life was influenced by my subconscious. Stories and labels that my mind has created when I was a kid, most of them fake, were controlling my reactions and choices and even health, which was a total game-changer. It is with this realization that reclaiming my power from those stories was the only way toward living a balanced and full life.

This inner work isn't a one-time effort; rather, it's a lifelong journey. Every step-whatever the size-generates transformation. Sometimes it feels like such a monumental shift, and sometimes it's almost imperceptible, but it's essential to keep moving, to continue peeling back these layers. It's a game without rules other than to keep going on, no matter how slow.

As I began to heal, I was able to perceive my experiences not as burdens but gifts. The dreams of my childhood to be a teacher, then a radio jockey, emerged in new forms. And in the world of coaching, I could fulfill the ultimate definition of teaching which was showing others their own paths. And then I was invited to be a guest speaker on Maharani Radio, and it became clear that even the childlike fascination with public speaking from my childhood had seeped into reality.

This understanding that whatever the distant dreams are, they will come into being eventually, really empowered me. This made me introspect also to the less pleasant ones. What about the problems, the fight, and the pain? Why are these happening? The reason behind this is our subconscious.

As a child, I would pretend to fall ill. It was not the disease or sickness that I sought after but the care and sympathy behind it. This tendency carried itself into adulthood with even different forms.When I was diagnosed with Asthma, all the care and attention I longed for was showered upon me while I basked in it. We do not realize how these unconscious behaviors drive our lives. They act more like an invisible thread-pulling in directions we never totally comprehend.

The journey to uncover these strands, to take back control of our lives was equally difficult and liberating. It involved becoming conscious, questioning one's story, and deliberately choosing other stories. And indeed, such a journey might never fully be complete because every single step brings on a deep sense of power and serenity that gives it worth.

It would be easy to look at each moment, good or bad, and see how they put me where I am now, or how the dots connected that otherwise, maybe a blind path. but all in their simplest form, the act of sharing, it has been healing, not only for me but also for the people I share it with. After all, sharing, as they say, is caring. And with these stories that we share, we create a ripple effect and touch lives in ways that we may never fully understand.

YOUR THOUGHTS

CHAPTER 3

(JUDGEMENT AND CRITICISM)

"*How do I allow life to flow with so many flaws?*" It is a question that has constantly been on my mind for as long as I can remember. Judgment and criticism, be it from within or others, have never left my side. I learned that these forces are always going to be a part of life, but that doesn't mean they dictate the way we live. My path to self-acceptance has been very drawn out and twisted around societal norms, family expectations, and the kind of relationship I am currently developing with myself.

A core part of being human is judgment. It is an almost instinctive human behavior; a way of making sense of the world by labeling and categorizing people, actions, and situations. Judgment is very useful if wielded constructively but if not, it turns out to be a prison of growth for the self and damaging for relationships. My encounters with judgment and criticism began early, with roots in what I experienced during childhood and adolescence. It wasn't until much later that I realized these patterns and decided to challenge them.

A Childhood Defined by Comparisons

My sister and I were the opposite sides of the same coin. My sister was the epitome of grace and poise, while I was the spirited tomboy. From early childhood, this contrast became the defining narrative between us. My mother would often point these contrasts out, of course with the best of intentions. It was a running joke in our family. My sister wore hair styled to perfection and dresses that were straight from the cleaner pressed neatly. I, instead, ran around in my shorts and t-shirts, often climbing trees with dirt on my face and speeding around on a white Vespa scooter.

I recall my mom always saying, "*Why can't you be more like your sister? Just look at her! Why can't you keep your hair neat like her? You should be a little more patient too.*" And though she spoke out of love, her words sowed seeds of inadequacy in me. I grew up thinking that I was never enough. Not patient enough, not feminine enough, not graceful enough. As I grew older, in my mind, I didn't realize when I started to compare myself with my sister too.

She was talented at things I could never even attempt, and my sense of value started becoming tied to how much like her I could be. During holidays when everybody returned home and gathered together for a meal, and the evening became a chaos filled with jokes and laughter, what stood out for me was relatives often saying things, quite unwittingly, that would just reinforce my self-doubt. "*Your sister is as graceful as ever*," they would say. I know they didn't mean to belittle me, but their remarks only made me feel unseen, as if my worth held no importance unless compared against hers.

Internalizing Judgments

These comparisons soon turned inside. I started to intensely scrutinize myself. All that I was, I constantly questioned - my clothes, my posture, my voice, even the way that I laughed. I felt how I picked apart everything about other people too, judging their decisions and looks. My mind incessantly calculated who was better and worse—never giving room to just be.

It was not just the external looks that were judged; it became a part of my thinking about my ability. At school, I was an excellent student but feared failure. I believed making even a slight error would prove that I was never good enough. This fear prevented me from being creative and losing a lot of opportunities.

I vividly remember my very first major academic failure, it was catastrophic like the world was ending. I completely blamed myself for that tragedy, internalized the setback as an affirmation of my inadequacy, and thought: "You see? You're not capable. You're just pretending."

Parenting Patterns: A Mirror to Ourselves

My early experience with my parents had played a huge role in sowing the seeds of deep-rooted self-criticism I had within me. My father, a strict disciplinarian, had high expectations from all of us. One vivid memory I can recall was when I was in second grade. A neighbor who happened to be a teacher asked me something in English. I didn't understand her at that time, and once she left, my dad was furious.

"*How do you not understand this simple English sentence?*" he had scolded. "*What people might think of my daughter who is studying in Air Force school?*"

His words that day had hurt me a lot. For the first time ever, I felt the burden of outer judgment. I started to see my failures and achievements as a reflection of my parents' reputation. It is something that has remained with me till date and reflects while I handle challenges. I asked for validation from teachers, friends, and even strangers. I felt that their approval was the same as my value.

Ironically, I followed in my father's footsteps as I grew older. I recall snapping at my younger brother for not being able to answer a question on a school visit. "What will my friends think?" I shouted without realizing that I too gradually became the same judge and critic that had created me.

The Invisible Cage of Labels

A lot of adults carry the labels chosen from childhood. These determine or create limiting beliefs based on how we view ourselves, coupled with what we perceive is the possibility of our being capable of achieving. Among such labels for me were -

moody/impatient

difficult/messy

unsophisticated

mediocre/not good enough

These become self-fulfilling prophecies, thus defining the choices we make—and avoid—and keeping us caught in cycles of doubt and fear.

Think about this. How often do we stay away from opportunities because fear of failure keeps us hushed? How many of us silence our voices, anticipating that no one is actually going to listen? This all comes from internalized judgments.

Awareness is the first step to freedom

Awareness is what can free one from the cycle of judgment. When we become aware of our thought processes, we automatically question those thoughts. For myself, it was something that developed gradually. I started to notice how frequently I judged myself and others. Why have I been so cruelly critical of myself when something or someone failed to meet deadlines or completed a tiny project? Why did I make such a big deal of other people's dressing, language, or how they behaved? The more that I looked at these trends the more I realized that at the bottom of it lay deep-seated fear about being rejected, fearing failures and never feeling worthy.

It was then that I met with the concept of self-compassion. I discovered that being gentle with myself was not a flaw but a necessity. I learned to affirm some of the following:

> I approve of myself.
>
> I am fine as I am.
>
> I release myself from the trappings of seeking external validation.

These affirmations did not overnight change my mindset, but they placed seeds of self-acceptance. And over the passage of time, I noticed the shift too.

The Ripple Effect of Self-Acceptance

This gave me a new way of dealing with people. I began to accept myself and slowly found that the need for comparison, whether it was with friends, colleagues, or family members, was fading away. I no longer had to be chained by insecurity, and thus I could really appreciate people for who they were, not shadowed by jealousy or competition.

Oftentimes judgments mirror our own fears and doubts. When I criticize others, it wasn't them; it was a part of me projecting my inner struggles. When I realized that, I turned inward with my insecurities instead of deflecting them outward into a judgment of others. From then on, there was this space for empathy and compassion not only towards others, but also towards myself.

I realized that once I started accepting myself, all sorts of things began changing about me. Energy in a relationship, interaction patterns and how much I open up to my friends and family; my assumptions started melting, no longer assuming the worst and always seeking to understand another person.

What's more, the ripple impact went beyond relationships. In the workplace, I was less defensive and more cooperative. When not driven by a need to prove myself, I found myself to be more present and solutions-focused.

Parenting with Awareness

Perhaps one of the greatest lessons that I learned is how my energy influences those around me, particularly children. Being a parent makes me realize very well how to use my words and intentions. I am no longer focusing on what I don't want them to do; instead, I'm emphasizing what I would like them to embrace.

For example, instead of saying, "*Don't mess up your room,*" I say, "*Let's keep the room clean so it's a happy space for all of us.*" All these small changes add to creating a positive mindset in them.

Children learn more by what we do than our words. They tend to mirror our energy. So, when we practice self-acceptance and love, we are giving permission to do the same to children.

The Role of Society in Perpetuating Judgment

No judgment talk can go without the mention of society's influence. We have been fed with messages since childhood on how we are supposed to present ourselves, behave, and even how we succeed. Social media adds to these impossible standards that very few people live up to. Perhaps the most liberating act was learning to disentangle myself from such expectations. I stopped comparing my life to those well-crafted photos online. I stopped seeking validation from those who never really knew me.

Letting go of judgment does not mean the abandonment of self-improvement. It only means shifting attention from criticism to growth. Instead of asking myself, "What the hell is wrong with me?" I began asking myself, "What can I learn from this?".

This mindset change changed my approach to challenges. Instead of fearing failure, I forced myself to embrace failure as part of growth.

As at the end of the day, it is our beliefs that determine our reality. If we believe we are worthless, we attract situations that will support that belief. If we believe in ourselves, we open ourselves up to opportunities. I have seen this principle work in my own life. I replaced self-doubt with self-confidence and achieved things that once seemed impossible.

Belief is not simply wishful thinking but the very base from which we operate and grow. To believe in ourselves changes both the way we view the world and how the world views us; it's a power, which when accessed, will unveil a myriad of possibilities.

A Life of Authenticity and Peace

I try to live authentically and not be bothered by judgment or criticism. Of course, that doesn't mean that I don't encounter my share of self-doubt or criticism. It is, after all, part of being human. Rather, it means that I learned how to respond to them elegantly and resiliently.

Self-acceptance, you see, is really a journey for life because once you learn to take of yourself, your virtues, and your weaknesses too, you become free to really live life on its fullest most jovial terms.

Judgments and criticisms will always be with us, but they don't need to define us. In the same breath, developing self-awareness, which practices self-compassion can free us from them. Let's look at each other with compassion, understanding, and kindness. Let's look at fear as something replaced by love, and instead of doubt, we hold onto belief.

The journey of self-acceptance is hard but transformative, in that it guides us through leaving our past, embracing our present, and stepping into a future filled full of possibilities.

YOUR THOUGHTS

CHAPTER 4

(POWER OF ACCEPTANCE)

The story of acceptance starts with a simple truth-life is what it is and not as we would like it to be. Liberating but challenging in many ways, this is a call for a very significant shift in mindset. Understanding acceptance requires an age-old wisdom as old as time itself, that teaches people how one should change what is possible and gracefully accept what is impossible. This chapter addresses the powerful effect of acceptance in our lives through reflections, relatable stories, and practical insights illuminating profound effects in living.

A Lesson from the Baby Parrot & Its Mommy

Once upon a time, there was a baby parrot looking longingly at the beautiful beaks of his friends, the swan and the pelican. "Why is my beak like this and not like theirs?" he asked his mother, pouting. "Why is it not so beautiful like theirs, mommy? I want pretty beaks like them too." The wise mother parrot smiled, shaking her head and explained to him calmly, "You are perfect, my baby. Your beak is a gift and just right for your body and the food that you eat. It's unique just like theirs."

But the baby parrot was stubborn and kept comparing himself with others wishing he had a pretty beak like his friends. That night, however, the angels heard him and a magic happened. His beak was transformed magically. It turned out to resemble that of the pelican's beak. The baby parrot was initially overjoyed, but he did not get to enjoy his newfound happiness for a long time. He soon discovered that he was unable to balance his head very well, and his favorite 'chilies and nuts' could no longer be gobbled with his new pretty beak. When his mommy gave him worms to eat, he cried miserably, missing his original beak and wanted it to be restored back to how it was before.

When the baby parrot awoke, it realized it was merely dreaming, but the lesson lingers: we are perfectly situated in life, designed for our roles. Comparing oneself with others only takes the joys and purposes from us to live our own lives.

Acceptance: A Path to Self-Awareness

The tale of the parrot is but the reflection of ourselves as human beings; we look at other people in order to see what we might be lacking and enlarge our strengths while diminishing ours. We forget that the circumstances in our lives— our parents, how we were raised, even our problems are not accidents but are a piece of the tapestry we call our lives. Acceptance begins with seeing life as it is, devoid of comparison or fantasy.

Think of an empty glass of water. It can be called half full or half empty, but acceptance allows us to think of it as simply that: a glass containing both water and space. All this clarity helps in understanding real life, accepting good and bad alike without a murmur.

Balancing Change and Acceptance

Life always seems to throw us a curveball that feels hard to accept like broken relationships, shattered dreams, countless wrongs. "*Why me?*" we ask in frustration. "*Why do terrible things happen if there's a God?*"

Acceptance is not the same as submitting to suffering. It's being aware that life plays according to a larger scheme of things. Everything—little and big, trivial and terrible—has a purpose. Shattering a plate, losing a relationship, or natural disasters are all pieces of the tapestry of existence.

It works by helping us find inner peace and clarity when challenged. Take, for instance, a woman in a troubled marriage. She spends every day of her life complaining and blaming fate. The reality, however, is that she possesses a lot of power. The power to choose. She may choose to stay and strive for understanding or leave to make a new life. But it is the fear of what is not known or perhaps what is known that often deters individuals. In this regard, acceptance involves allowing the situation to be, recognizing options, and making a choice rather than living as a victim. Acceptance is not passive; instead, it is an action to accept reality, including the courage to make it better if possible.

The Bigger Picture: Life's Balance of Good and Bad

Acceptance extends beyond individual challenges to the complexities of the world. We are also disturbed by the presence of evil—corruption, violence, or injustice. As day gives way to night, so does good in its coexistence with bad find a balance that gives meaning to life. Without sorrow, we would not appreciate joy. Without darkness, we would not appreciate light.

Our emotions also reflect this duality. Happiness, love, and gratitude coexist with jealousy, fear, and guilt. Acceptance enables us to transform even the otherwise destructive emotions into energies to facilitate growth and change.

Acceptance is not a destination but a journey. It requires practice and mindfulness. Here are some steps that can help develop this important skill:

1. Identify Your Emotions

Start by recognizing your emotions without judgment. Whether it is anger, sadness, or fear, just recognition and acceptance of your emotion are the first steps in achieving clarity.

2. List Your Struggles

Come up with a list of situations or aspects of life that you cannot accept. Then explore why these situations are hard to accept and what makes them matter to you.

3. Evaluate Your Values

Reflect on what is currently in conflict with your core beliefs. The point of understanding this discrepancy between your values and current reality is that it could prove what needs to be different.

4. Act Where Possible

Identify what can be changed and do something about it. Change is very much a slow process, but it does have to start with obvious intentions and tiny actions.

5. Let Go of the Unchangeable

For things that are out of your hands in life, learn to accept. It doesn't mean the end; it means to let go of the unnecessary friction.

Self-Love starts with Accepting Yourself and Others

Acceptance begins at the self. We are often our own worst critics when we tell ourselves that we are lacking in certain areas. That self-bashing lowers our self-worth while hindering our personal growth. In fact, one needs to begin treating oneself like how you would treat a good friend.

Self-love is embracing yourself just the way you are - completely unfiltered. It is accepting both the strengths and weaknesses. It is accepting our mistakes guilt-free and knowing that failure is just a lesson in disguise. When we don't compare ourselves to others and accept our own journey, we unlock freedom to grow and thrive.

Just as we need to accept ourselves, we also have to extend acceptance to others. Human beings are fashioned by what they have experienced or believe and circumstances. When we start judging others or force them to turn into the ideal, this causes conflict.

Think of an example like your friend or a neighbor rushes by you without saying goodbye. Instead of assuming them being rude, think of another possible answer. They might have had something on their mind or they were running late. This change in perspective can result in anger becoming understanding and making relationships stronger.

The need for acceptance of others involves having empathy and a willingness to see things from the perspective of another. It does not necessarily condone their behavior but shows understanding in knowing that everybody has their own path and struggle.

This world, despite all its flaws and paradoxes, holds some valuable lessons for anyone willing to observe and learn. It is easy to desire a utopia devoid of pain, but life in the real world is more complex than that. Pain and joy, darkness and light, coexist for the depth and meaning of life. The way of moving through this duality is by accepting—a practice that lets one embrace the world as it is and find ways to make a positive contribution to it.

Life never fails to test our faith in fairness. Earthquakes, inequality, and personal failures make life seem cruel and unrelenting. Yet, there is a reason why these trials befall us. They test our resiliency, foster growth, and teach us compassion. If we can accept the world as not perfect, we can move beyond the pain of the moment and find the unnoticed lessons, which adversity holds within itself.

Life's fundamental truth is that "your thoughts create your reality." If we decide the world is cruel and unfair to us, then negativity becomes our self-fulfilling prophecy. Anger and frustration obscure our vision such that we cannot see through to the good that happens. On the other hand, having a grateful and positive attitude attracts positivity. It doesn't mean not seeing the problems in the world but facing them with the possibility of change and growth.

Acceptance of the world also includes its natural equilibrium and duality. For instance, the conical shape of the trees in the hills shows how their environment has shaped them so that they can sustain themselves under heavy snow. Each natural element is fashioned according to its surroundings, thereby implying that even the most volatile systems have an intrinsic order. This allows us to observe that everything in life has a reason and a place, though perhaps it is not readily noticeable.

With such universal truth aligned in our minds, we will develop inner peace and strength. Acceptance enables us to give up the futile fight against things we cannot change and to free our energy to concentrate on what we can control. It gives us the power to be an active agent for making the world a better place to live, beginning with ourselves.

At its core, acceptance of the world is not a complacent attitude but one that brings harmony. It acknowledges the beauty in imperfection and finds meaning in chaos; it strives to be the light in a very complicated and ever-changing reality.

Practice Acceptance

As with any skill, acceptance needs practice. Here are a few exercises to help put acceptance into everyday life -

1. Distinguish Reality from Fantasy

Reflect on your expectations and where they fail to match reality. Such an awareness brings with it less frustration and a whole lot of gratitude.

2. Embrace Mistakes

Rather than dwelling on mistakes, embrace them as a means of growth. Learn to Celebrate the lessons they bring and move forward with renewed understanding.

3. Practice Gratitude

Pay attention to the best things about your life. The regular expression of thankfulness shifts the perspective from lack to abundance.

4. Practice Mindfulness

Be mindful of the moment, taking in life without judgment. Mindfulness quiets the internal chatter and promotes acceptance.

5. Utilize Affirmations

Repeating affirmations, such as "*I accept my life fully and completely,*" cultivates an acceptance mentality.

The Power of Acceptance: A Universal Law

And you see, acceptance isn't just a personal virtue; it's a universal law. Life happens as it should, much like a blockbuster movie in which we all have a role to play. Each person we meet and every incident we face is part of our journey.

When we start accepting ourselves and others the way we are, that is where we let go of resistance and flow into peacefulness. We become heroes, the authors of our stories who can write our reality as we want it, not as we fear it.

As we come to the last step of this journey, envision standing at the edge of a serene lake. The water is not perfectly still-its ripples reflect light and shadows from the sky above. Acceptance is, in some way, looking into that lake and appreciating what it is there for instead of wishing it were quieter, clearer, or any other way altogether. And it's an art through which life unfolds, embracing it in its messiness, imperfections, and seeking beauty in raw, unfettered truth.

YOUR THOUGHTS

CHAPTER 5

(FORGIVENESS)

Forgiveness is a very gentle act of power. It is not just a reaction to wrongdoing or the resolution of interpersonal conflicts. In truth, it is a deliberate choice, an act of love born within. Like Lewis B. Smedes rightly said, *"To forgive is to set a prisoner free and discover that the prisoner was you."* Forgiveness uncovers the chains that restrain us from experiences like pain, anger, and resentment, it then helps our hearts and minds to heal and grow.

One might believe that forgiveness is a means to excuse or nullify what another has done, to erase the past. But it is far from it. To me, it is more of a personal journey, a deliberate process if I may say. One of letting go the negatives and grudges we hold within ourselves. It kind of detoxifies the mind and body. And in doing so, an understanding with ourselves and what goes on around us is obtained. Forgiveness is when we abandon anger or resentment towards offenders so that not only are we taking away the punishment due but, more importantly, ourselves are freed from the very burdens we carry.

The Nature of Forgiveness

This would simply mean that acknowledging its complexity makes up the foundation of how one understands the idea of letting go. It's not a singular action; rather, it's this multi-layered process, one akin to peeling an onion; one layer brings upon another layer of emotions and understanding. At the heart of it, it is recognizing harm, processing the deep feelings, and then consciously deciding to let go of the pain related to it.

Let's consider the story of a young woman who is burdened with a deep seated grudge against a former childhood friend who betrayed her trust. She stayed away from thoughts of the incident for years thinking she had left it in the past. Meanwhile, this unresolved anger was stealthily governing her relationships because she would not readily give someone her all. That particular betrayal had pushed her to develop trust issues. Eventually, through journaling and therapy, she confronted her emotions by reliving the pain while gaining clarity in the process. She realized that it was not malice but insecurities in her friend that led to the betrayal. This new perspective provided a window of opportunity whereby she was able to clear herself of the resentment, not for the benefit of her friend, but for herself. Through this, she found that she was now more receptive to deep connections.

The process of letting go of resentment is often accompanied by a complicated cocktail of emotions that usually encompasses sadness, bitterness, and sometimes even rage. At such times, it may be hard to find that elusive empathy and understanding but in choosing to let go of anger, we make room for compassion. This change is as much about extending grace to others as it is about self-awareness. For instance, a father and son were stuck in a cycle of argument and misunderstanding for years. The son felt choked under constant criticism and was harboring anger in every interaction they had. It was over one very intense conversation, when he blurted out to his father, "*You never believed in me!*" But when his father shot back with, "*I only pushed you because I didn't want you to struggle like I did,*" things began to change. It was the mutual vulnerability that allowed the two to finally look through their resentments and, with mutual respect, work on building their bond back.

Similar to the development of any good behavior, this is an effort that demands consistency and patience. Developing the habit of emotional release requires facing the truth of uncomfortable things. Consider the case of a manager who harbored resentment towards his colleague for stealing an idea of his. The initial response to this situation was of course tension and avoidance. But when the manager decided to openly tackle the issue after some reflections, the colleague, in surprise, admitted to doing wrong and shared fears about being overlooked. This conversation, full of honesty, relaxed the tension and came out with a valuable lesson that healing and better relationships might come from addressing a grievance directly.

Releasing resentment is not a justification of bad behavior or an excuse for it. Rather, it is a personal decision to break free from the burden of carrying anger and bitterness around. This is an act of self-liberation, allowing for peace and the ability to learn. Every step forward, no matter how painful, is another step toward becoming a lighter, freer self.

The Psychology Behind Forgiveness

From a psychological point of view, releasing resentment leads to emotional healing, reduced stress, good mental health, and better relationships between individuals involved and those letting go. And what else does one crave if not mental peace, right? Here are some key aspects -

1. Emotional Healing

Holding anger and hatred causes emotional wounds that grow in strength over time. Unforgiveness can cause stress, anxiety, and even depression. Deciding to forgive heals those emotional wounds, reduces the degree of negative emotions, and cultivates an inner sense of peace.

2. Empathy and Perspective

Forgiveness needs us to seek the human side in anyone who has hurt us. This helps with empathy, since by trying to understand why they acted so or struggling with themselves makes us more empathetic and promotes compassion and growth in the personality.

3. Letting go of resentment.

Resentment is an emotional anchor which keeps us attached to the pain and bitterness. Forgiveness is an active process of working through these emotions until we have released their hold on our lives. Forgiveness is not forgetting but choosing better than vengeance.

4. Rebuilding Relationships

Forgiveness is not necessarily reconciliation; it sets the way for rebuilt trust and closer relationships. Forgiveness creates the opportunity for both of the parties involved to grow in each other's lives and better understand each other even when a relationship may seem unrepairable.

5. Self-Forgiveness

Perhaps the most difficult yet necessary step in the act of forgiveness is self-forgiveness. Whether it is guilt, regret, or self-blame, self-forgiveness is a crucial step towards emotional freedom. It empowers us to accept ourselves as human beings, imperfections and all, and carry on with renewed strength.

The Transformative Power of Forgiveness

Forgiveness is an ultimate healer that not only works at the emotional level, but also impacts our vision and perception of self and of the world around us. It is, indeed, a transformative process requiring one to go through introspection, love for self, and spiritual growth. And still, many individuals shun this road, usually subconsciously. This is reflected in denial and self-blame. When asked, *"Do you forgive yourself?"* the responses typically fall into two categories:

The Denial: To some, forgiveness is a concept that does not apply to them since they do not feel that they have done anything wrong. In such cases, they will often deny the need to confront their feelings and past deeds. "*Why should I forgive? Nothing wrong has been done by me*" is their rhetorical question. This approach may spring from a deep-felt fear of vulnerability. It would demand them to go through painful emotions that they'd rather avoid. Layers of their inner selves are left untouched, for fear of what they may find. In the avoidance of self-reflection, they lose out on deep healing by letting go of emotional burdens and embracing compassion towards themselves.

The Self-Blamers: On the other extreme are those who take to heart all the mistakes, misunderstandings, and conflicts as if they themselves were responsible for them. "Everything that goes wrong is my fault," they might say. This self-blaming tendency mostly stems from deep-rooted guilt. A person does not consider himself worthy of accepting his imperfections, and he fails to understand that life is a balance between choices, circumstances, and external factors, which sometimes are out of their hands. Thus, the individual cannot forgive himself for his mistakes committed in the past, as a result of which he remains behind and keeps punishing himself within this vicious cycle.

Denial and self-blame represent both a lack of self-compassion and the inability to recognize the inherent value within ourselves. We are not here to please others or to be worthy of living up to other people's expectations; we are here for a reason the universe set out for us on this journey. Our souls are important, and that is why we should find our way, learn our lessons, and experience life that is uniquely ours. As we forgive ourselves, we also honor our existence, our journeys, and our worth. Forgiveness is being able to let go of a past and embracing the fuller version of who we truly are, together with our flaws and imperfections. It is simply understanding that our mistakes and wrongs do not form our identity, and our values are inherent, not defined by our actions.

Steps to Self-Forgiveness

To achieve self-forgiveness and ultimately personal transformation, one must navigate the following steps:

> **Forgive yourself**
>
> You might start by being honest about the ways you've been harmful to yourself-be it through bad habits, self-neglect, or harsh self-judgment. Activities that can be pleasantly cathartic may include writing forgiveness letters or even just saying affirmations.
>
> **Affirmations**
>
> Repeat, "I am willing to forgive myself," while doing deep breathing. Repetition is the process of rewiring the subconscious mind, so that new, positive beliefs are imprinted.
>
> **Write a letter.**
>
> Write down all of that which you want to forgive yourself for. Think as to why you acted in the particular way you did and give them

another meaning. Burn it - it is a symbolic act of guilt leaving one's body.

Forgiving Your Parents

Many of our childhood complaints emanate from misunderstandings. Sometimes, as children, we may have misinterpreted kind intentions, and the subconscious mind locked away grudges. Acknowledging that our parents are human and struggling in their ways can help us let go of these grievances.

Begin with easy **affirmations** such as:

> "I am ready to forgive my parents."
>
> "I want to let go of all the resentment I have towards my parents."

For your healing to be further nurtured, try this **activity** -

> Write a letter of forgiveness about some specific memories to your parents.
>
> Burn the letter, letting go of the past.

Forgiving Others and Incidents

Life is full of experiences that try to break our forgiving nature. Keeping resentment for these things just digs us into the ground of the past. Find those people or situations that wronged you and deliberately decide to forgive them. It is not that you are approving what they did, but you are letting go of their emotional control over you.

Begin this process with a simple **affirmation:**

"I am willing to forgive…"

Deepen this practice with the **activity** below:

Write a letter to the person or situation that hurt you. Go on and express all emotions, thoughts, and grievances.

Burn the letter, and let its flames symbolize the end of your pain and anger.

Seeking Forgiveness

It takes bravery to seek forgiveness because it leads to healing not only for you but also for others. Humility and accepting the actions are the greatest components of remorse. Sincere regret with apologies reveals growth, making the one wronged know his pain matters. Forgiveness is not guaranteed, but the act of asking for it is transformative. It allows you to unburden yourself of guilt and move on. It makes your character stronger, brings accountability, and then opens up to more honest, deeper connections. Seeking forgiveness is just as much about growth as it is about repairing relationships.

A Liberating Journey

Forgiveness is freedom; it is an act of boldness, of choosing between love over hate, peace over conflict, and growth over stagnation. It is a process which requires time, effort, and unrelenting commitment toward self-betterment.

You need to understand that forgiveness is not forgetting and definitely not excusing, but taking back your power so you are free from the fetters of pain and then going on to create life that is full of love, care, and happiness.

Forgiveness is not an action but a way of living—it is the path towards actual freedom.

Let it mold you into your true self.

YOUR THOUGHTS

CHAPTER 6

(THE POWER OF INTENTION)

Think of planting a small seed. You watch it grow, tend it, water it, let it get sunlight; gradually, it turns out into a thriving plant. Here is how the above applies to the power of your intentions. Your intention forms and shapes your future into everything that is going on inside your life. Whether we're aware of it or not, every step we take actually starts as an intention. With awareness and mastery over this ability, we align with the best possible expressions of our potential and, by extension, bring flow where we feel stuck.

The Energy Behind Intention

Intention is not an ephemeral thought or wishing; it's an energized direction. By making an intention, one channels energy toward the fulfillment of that intention and allows it to grow until it materializes. For instance, the intention set while practicing yoga, is being fit, but it channels in energy toward the overall well-being too. In contrast, yoga practice to lose weight is targeted towards a particular result. The difference between the outcomes is in the intention for the action.

The power of Intention is considered so strong because it wakes up forces within that lie dormant in the person otherwise. Most people tend to miss this power or brush it off as being too mundane. For others, the idea seems vague or intangible. But intention is not some outside force; it is an inborn gift. We just need to evoke it and tap into our consciousness and our inner selves.

Intention as a Connection

Imagine a quiet evening wherein Meha, a budding artist, sits by the window, sketching for hours. For years she got no recognition for it. She painted not for her own pleasure but to get into the expectations of other people, trendy colors and popular themes. She kept trying, but it did not feel right as if there's always something or the other missing. Her art didn't feel like it came from her soul.

One day, her mentor asked, "Why do you paint?" Meha stilled for a moment, that question made her realize that she did not have an answer. Her mentor just smiled and said, "Before you start picking up your brush, first set an intention. Not for others but for yourself. Let the heart decide your way.

That night, Meha sat with her sketchbook. She shut her eyes and asked herself not what would sell or gather likes but, "What do I really want my art to convey?" And from the intent came her creation—pouring all the emotion she had into that which was going to reflect her own soul.

With this clear understanding, Meha produced her first artwork with intent. It turned out wonderful-not just in appearance, but in energy. Authenticity emanated from it, drawing people in like a magnet. She realized for the first time how she could relate to her own self through her passion.

Intention, Meha learned, is not just a goal. It is a connection, a bridge, perhaps between inner awareness and infinite possibilities in the universe; it's knowing who you are and aligning with what you want on the basis of that knowledge.

Setting an intention opens up an energy channel, like Meha did, that naturally flows. The universe listens to our clarity, allowing us to manifest our dreams. However, such connection requires trust. When Meha let go of her self-doubt and kept the focus on her essence, her art and life blossomed, reminding her that true fulfillment begins from when intention aligns with authenticity.

The Role of Ego

Amongst the biggest problems of getting to tap on the intention power is that of the ego. The term 'ego' in simple terminology comes from the acronym "Edging God Out", which discharges one out of love. Ego creates space for pride and comparison, little space being left for one's self-importance with no intention present.

Ego makes us define ourselves through the following external parameters like:

I am what I am: Ego attaches identity to the body, ignoring the fact that the soul is infinite.

I am what I do: The accomplishments and the titles become the basis for self-esteem, and inner happiness is neglected.

I am what others think of me: Society's reputation defines who we are, and we end up living for others.

I am separated from all: Ego creates a separation that splits us from the unity of life.

I am separate from what is missing: This perception feeds lack, causing us not to embrace fullness.

I am separate from God: Ego splits us off from the divine, leaving us feeling less than worthy of divine love.

Despite the fact that ego is just a three-letter word, it has the most overwhelming influence on human life. It makes people feel significant, yet reduces their vision. In the lives of individuals governed by ego, everything becomes about their success and acquisitions, at the cost of peace of mind.

Rising Above Ego

To become active in our intention fully, we need to rise above our ego. It does not mean negating individuality rather it is about accepting the fact that we are much more than our accomplishments, possessions, or names. Letting go of the ego gives us room for love—the true form of life.

For example, a person may be very successful professionally but yet feel a lingering dissatisfaction. His ego would tell him that he was only valuable because of his title or the amount of money he earns. But if he turns inward and sets an intention to grow, he will find fulfillment beyond material success.

The process of rising above ego requires a conscious decision for self-worth to be readjusted. Instead of, "*What do I own?*" or "*What do others perceive of me?*" we can ask, "*Who am I with all these external definitions?*" Once this shift in perspective is felt, we connect with the higher self, where everything intended blooms.

Practical Steps to Harness Intention

Set Clear Intentions

Start with clarity: ask yourself what you would really like and why. For instance, if you are moving careers, is it that you need to grow as a professional, have a better work-life balance, or achieve higher financial stability? Define your intention and visualize yourself confidently in that role.

Let Go of Self-Doubt

Doubt dilutes intention. Believe in your ability to make your dream life a reality. Affirmations such as "I can achieve what I want to" will help to replace doubt with belief.

Align Actions to Intentions

It's like a seed without soil: intentions without action are meaningless. Take steps towards your goal, whether that's learning a new skill, networking, or just a good attitude.

Practice Gratitude

Gratitude actually strengthens the intention by focusing your mind away from what's lacking toward what is available. Relish in what you've accomplished and what is still in front of you, creating an abundance and positive mindset.

Detach from Expecting Outcomes

While it is in the nature of things to have expectations, attachment creates frustration. Focus on the journey and trust that the universe would put things right for you.

Let's See Some Real-Life Examples

Let us consider this strong-willed woman, Maya, a single mother with two children, working a stressful job. She feels like her life is in an endless loop she is stuck in where even a moment of respite is a luxury, rushing through each day in hopes of somehow making it without falling apart. She says to herself she is "making ends meet," but deep down inside, she knows that it just cannot continue like this. One night, tired and tear-stained, she comes across a journal she had bought months earlier. On impulse, she writes down her goals: "*I want to have a peaceful, loving home for my kids and find balance in my life.*"

At first, it sounded stupid to Maya. How would the writing of a sentence possibly alter her reality? But over the days, she sees some changes that are tiny in nature. Instead of shouting at her kids at breakfast time, she now puts on soft music. She draws boundaries in the workplace so that most evenings she gets home on time for dinner. Gradually, the intent of having a peaceful ambiance begins to manifest. Maya starts to make decisions that match the goal through her new clarity.

The point is that Maya was not looking to just end her immediate struggle but rather find what she truly wanted, which is peace, connection, and balance. Clarity like that changes the direction of her activities and priorities and gets her closer to an ideal life.

Now think of Rohan, a man in his mid-forties who has been suffering with his back pain for decades. He tried every remedy others have advised him, beginning from some medicines to bodily therapies and even as far as undergoing surgeries, but nothing appeared to work on him for a long period. Feeling frustrated and resigned, Rahul starts practicing yoga, hoping it might bring some relief. Initially, his intention is to not experience pain. But as he progresses, he starts setting another intention: "I want to feel strong and healthy."

This switch flips everything around. Now he celebrates small victories like how he can touch his toes, or he can sleep comfortably without pain. Positive thought pushes him further to research other habits that are also supportive of his health. He finds that he should improve his diet and walk daily. With time, Rahul transforms his relationship with his body from just managing pain. His new intention, therefore, based on strength and vitality, helps him regain power over his life.

Why Do These Examples Matter?

Both Maya and Rohan began with struggles that seemed like mountains to climb. And they could have easily ended up stuck in those respective cycles of stress and pain forever. But by setting clear intentions, they tapped into the magic of focus and alignment, which changed everything. No magic, no wish fulfillment, but rather using this energy within to make this change.

The beauty of intention, I think, is really in the way it switches perspective. It's about not just what you want but why you want it, and when you find this deeper "why," naturally, your actions will align with your goals; and the universe seems to work for you.

So, no matter whether in regards to seeking peace in the relationships, healing in one's body, or clarification in one's life, all begin with intention. You have the power, like Maya and Rohan, to transform your story, one intention at a time.

Intention: A Path to Flow

When we are aligned with our higher self, we experience flow: a state in which life flows effortlessly. This doesn't mean that challenges will not come but that we face them with clarity, resilience, and purpose.

Intention will connect us to the power of the universe that oversees all creation. By allowing that power to flow within and through us, not only do we sculpt our future and lead us to discover who we truly are. Let the compass of intention guide you into transformation in not just what you do, but who you become.

YOUR THOUGHTS

CHAPTER 7

(INTUITION)

We all had moments when we 'just know' something without knowing why or how we know it. I used to think it was some superpower I had until I realized a lot of other people possessed that power too. Upon researching further, I learnt that it's called 'intuition'. It is a subtle yet mighty force that guides us past logic or conscious thought. It differs a lot from instinct and also rational thinking, as in logic-based thoughts, which need reasoning, arguments, and evidence for logical judgments. Intuition, for that matter, comes from the deep within; a whisper that creates a sense of connection with oneself as well as with deeper aspects and energy around.

It's all about recognizing and honing intuition that can help one with growth in the personality, with regard to making decisions, and, most importantly, in the face of uncertainty in life. That is, having an inner compass which keeps pointing a person toward paths aligned with their true purpose.

Understanding Intuition

Intuition is deeply personal and versatile, a phenomenon that manifests in ways resonating uniquely with each person. Understanding these different forms of intuition can help us recognize and trust that subtle inner guide.

Gut Instinct

Often referred to as a "*gut feeling*" or "*feeling in your stomach*," gut instinct is the body's intuition of whether something is right or wrong. It arises in the enteric nervous system sometimes called the "second brain. It is not just an emotional response, but a complex process in which we automatically evaluate slight cues with the assessment of previous experiences. Just think about when you first met someone and, suddenly, you felt you trusted them or didn't. That was your gut intuition working for you by giving non-verbal signals and showing you patterns at subconscious levels.

Emotional Intuition

This kind of intuition makes you attuned to both your and other people's feelings. It lets you know unseen emotions and their origins. For instance, you may know a friend is upset despite telling you that everything's alright. Emotional intuition closes gaps in communication, thus increasing the ability to empathize with each other.

Mental Intuition

Mental intuition can be described as that defining characteristic when a sudden insight or idea appears out of nowhere in your mind. It is like a lightbulb moment, the kind where the answer to a question just seems to pop up in your mind. Usually, such insights have resulted from the background processing your brain is doing. Solving a problem hours—or even days—after moving away from it because your subconscious has been working in the background is an excellent example of this.

Spiritual Intuition

This deep type of intuition links you with something more than yourself; it might be called higher power, universal energy, or inner wisdom. Spiritual intuition is the voice that usually appears as alignment or guidance towards paths that feel very meaningful. It is the inner voice nudging you towards dreams or transformation, even if it seems to go against logic.

Through understanding these forms of intuition, you are able to make better decisions, deepen your relationships, and navigate through life in a more coherent way.

How Intuition Works

The science behind Intuition is very interesting, stemming from the subconscious mind and processes way faster than that of conscious awareness. Even emotions and energy play their roles—the reason intuition often presents itself is due to minor shifts in energy or subtle emotional cues the brain interprets as a concrete insight.

Neuroscience has proven that the brain constructs intuitive knowledge out of past experiences, emotions, and sensory input with the help of its neural networks. It's not magic; it's just the way our brain gathers immense amounts of information in milliseconds of thinking.

Developing & Practicing Intuition

Practicing Mindfulness

Intuition, in fact, can only enter the mind once everyday noise is hushed. This can be achieved through mindfulness as given below:

> **Meditation:** A few minutes each day of focused breathing help keep one aware.
>
> **Journaling:** Going through experiences will give an insight into the pattern created by intuition.
>
> **Connectivity with Nature:** Staying outside more often helps a person in tuning to the rhythm of nature and themselves.

Trust Your Inner Voice

Self-doubt drowns out intuition very often. Learn to trust your inner voice.

> **Self-Doubt:** Observe and acknowledge it without judgment.
>
> **Develop Confidence:** Engage with intuitive decisions made for simple things and experience the outcomes.
>
> **Fear versus Intuition:** Your intuition usually feels calm and sure while your fear could feel suffocating and reactive.

Intuition-Building Exercises

Activities to Develop Your Intuition

> **Intuitive Meditations:** Imagine a situation and concentrate on the feelings it gives you, not the overthinking process.
>
> **Creative Expression:** Draw, paint, or write without thinking much; your creative products might express intuitive ideas.
>
> **Trust-Building Exercises:** Trust a gut feeling about some small, low-risk decision.

Applying Intuition in Daily Life

Decision-Making

Intuition is a great tool in navigating complex choices. As much as rational pros-and-cons lists are helpful, listening to your intuitive sense can often clarify things. Take the example of choosing a new job: the number on the paycheck is important, but intuition might be what guides you to the environment where you'll thrive.

Relationships and Communication

Intuition will be able to strengthen your relationship by tuning into how and what someone's energy feels like or their intentions. Have you ever felt your friend was upset before they even uttered a word? This, my dear reader, is called emotional intuition in action, helping you find solutions through empathy and closer connections.

Personal Growth and Transformation

Intuition is able to steer you toward passions and life changes that can connect with the 'authentic' you. An activity that gives you pleasure can become a career option when you listen to that little voice inside of you.

Overcoming Challenges & Doubts

Although the journey of development and cultivation of trusting your intuition might be fulfilling; however, it is far from being easy. All humans face some problems that provoke hesitation or uncertainty. In fact, it is important to know such challenges and understand how to overcome them in order to have a good relationship with inner guidance.

Common Problems

Self-Doubt

One of the biggest obstacles when it comes to intuition is you second-guessing it. You might dismiss the slight nudges as irrational or not important, especially when they go against logic or the outside advice. This will create self-doubt, which will prevent you from acting on valuable insights.

Fear of Mistakes

The fear that you will make the wrong decision causes you to overthink or hesitate. You may dread that, in relying too much on intuition, this may result in errors or unwanted output, so you question its validity.

Distinguishing signals

Another common challenge is confusing intuition with personal desires, fears, or biases. It is sometimes very difficult to determine whether a feeling should be considered intuitive or emotional.

Building Resilience

Practice self-compassion

Accept that mistakes happen and that is a way of growing. Be nice to yourself when your instincts don't go as expected. Avoid being judgmental about what has happened and focus instead on what has been learned.

Reframe Failures

View mistakes as lessons for improving your instincts. Each experience, failure and success, teaches you better understanding of your inner cues and helps you build on them as a basis for trusting yourself.

Cultivate a growth mindset

Believe in your ability to get better. Intuition, like every kind of skill, takes practice and hard work to develop. Accept challenges as opportunities for growth, reminding yourself that each step is progress, no matter how small it is.

By facing them head-strong with practice and most importantly patience, confidence in intuition eventually surfaces for you to guide yourself, despite the complexities that occur around you.

Intuition in Action: A Real-Life Example

Imagine Raya, a young woman in her late twenties having a midlife crisis. She is torn between whether to stay in her stable 9-5 corporate job or go for her childhood dream of pursuing photography. Her rational mind goes through a list of risks: insecurity regarding finance in the future, little experience and the most important one - societal pressures. Yet her intuition whispers to her softly, "This is your calling. You've always wanted this."

Rather than a spur-of-the-moment decision, she chooses ways to be guided intuitively—for instance, starting a photography blog, attending workshops, and slowly, gradually building a portfolio. It is with time that these intuitive moves will propel a booming career that fills her with happiness and brings success.

Conclusion

Intuition is a gift in all of us, but with trust and nurturing, it can be fully developed. Start by cultivating mindfulness, listening to the inner voice, and allowing intuition to guide you every day in your decisions.

Reflect on those instances when your intuition guided you—how did it feel?

For more in-depth knowledge on intuition, you can refer to books, courses, or guided meditations available online. The important thing to realize when it comes to intuition is that it is not a tool; it is a bridge to your authentic self that leads to a life of fulfillment.

YOUR THOUGHTS

CHAPTER 8

(THE POWER OF SILENCE)

In today's fast paced world that is humming and buzzing constantly, the concepts of silence and pause have become a long forgotten art form. Surrounded by constant notifications, daily chatter, and unspoken expectations to be occupied with constant activity, silence and pause became overlooked aspects. What if, instead of finding the real strength in activities themselves, one found it between those gaps? What if that space is not void that must be avoided but rather treasured?

The Essence of Silence & Pause

Silence and pause, though highly interrelated, have very different functions and purposes that bring distinctive value to life. Silence can be defined as the absence of noise from outside—a tranquil moment where the clamor of the world recedes into the background, leaving peace and clarity behind. It is a kind of an escapade from persistent noise and stimulus, which seems to overwhelm all of our senses constantly. Amidst this quietness, an individual finds comfort and space where they can rediscover their inner self and focus more on their thought processes.

On the other hand, pause is an active choice. It's a decision to stop and catch your breath so you have room to think and reflect before the next move. It enables people to be in the moment and to judge the point where they are so they can be deliberate in their actions. It's not just a break but an alert moment of being aware and aligning oneself with one's consciousness.

Envision yourself at the edge of a serene lake just as dawn begins to rise. The world, it seems, holds its breath—the water is still, there is a soft rustling of leaves, and for this brief moment, time has been arrested just for you. That's silence for you — a gift of stillness that beckons you inside and away from all distractions into the heart of a moment. Now, imagine stepping into a library. Within it, silence takes a whole different role. Absence of chattering creates sanctuaries where focus and deeper reflection can be made so that thoughts run free and get shaped without disruption.

Now, compare that to the effect of a conscious pause. Picture being in the middle of an intense argument, emotions raging, and words wanting to spill out. But you don't do that. You stop. You breathe deeply, give yourself a moment to reflect on what step to take, and you take great care in choosing what to say next. It's that brief moment that changes the whole conversation from argument to understanding.

Silence settles life and pause readies us for movement. The moments they intertwine are the ones that lend rhythm and depth to life.

Think of life like a well-written piece of music. The sounds are the deeds, the dialogue, and happenings of life. Without rests, the silences and pauses in the music, it would become a mess and not even remotely rhythmic. These moments of silence are what keeps the balance, allowing us to soak in the melody, appreciate the subtleties, and get ourselves ready again for the next note. Silence and pause are the hidden treasures that give life its depth and richness.

Finding Joy in the Stillness In A Noisy World

Life these days has become so very busy, isn't it? All these social networks are constantly asking for our time. Conversations are overlapping each other, and even moments set for rest get spent before the screen. Silence is considered awkward to be filled with some noise or some activity. But in this steady din, it is silence which is balm—a sacred space where our mind can breathe again and our souls reconnect.

How long has it been since you really sat in silence? No soft music playing in the background, no scrolling through your phone for what feels like an eternity, no rushing to fill up the space with noise or activity? In today's fast-paced, always-connected world, pure silence is a luxury few can afford, but it holds incredible power.

It is in the quiet, unsullied air of these kinds of spaces where clarity often re-emerges almost magically. Without so many distractions out there pulling our strings in hundreds of different ways, we sit down, left alone to our thoughts and feelings and sense of self. This slow, gentle quietness sows fertile soil for self-realization, to the point of truths and discoveries surfacing on the surface.

It is important to realize that silence is not a void but a canvas. It is the natural state of life in which inner wisdom makes its loudest noises often nudging us toward understanding, resolution, and even change.

The Transformative Benefits of Silence and Pause

Silence and pause do hold the transformative power for all things in our life.

Lowering Stress and Anxiety

Life is, sometimes, like running a race; our thoughts run at maximum speed. The quietness, on the other hand, slows it down, thus making the noises in our head settle. Studies have proven that periods of silence can decrease the levels of cortisol, hence decreasing stress and promoting relaxation. For me, taking a pause for five minutes in the middle of a chaotic day has always felt like my brain hitting a reset button.

Improving Focus and Concentration

I always try to pause before tackling something, when distractions fade & everything is silent, I have realized my mind works the best. Silence actually helps us realize our full mental potential by placing our focus rightly on the immediate present. For this reason alone, silence tends to enhance all productivity and judgment.

Encouraging Innovation and Creativity

Most of the best ideas are born in silence. You must know that some of your best ideas come to you when you're in the shower, walking alone, or staring out the window right? It happens a lot to me. Such times of quiet enable our subconscious to connect the dots and come up with new things.

Improve Self-awareness and self-reflection

Silence provides space to think. Such silent moments make us listen more closely to ourselves. For instance, journaling in silence periods has been something of a breakthrough for me, things have finally made sense about myself and in navigating life generally.

The Pause That Changes Conversations

A pause is indeed very powerful in communication. A perfect pause may help one think through what would best be said and then respond, giving scope for true understanding. It encourages listening, avoids impulsive reactions, and shows respect. In conversations, pause is what can turn them into opportunities for connections, empathy, and meaningful dialogues.

Active listening

How many times do we listen just to respond instead of trying to understand? When we pause in a conversation, we are able to really listen to the other person and empathize with them even more deeply. There was one conversation I had with my very close friend; I remember simply pausing to listen shifted the course of our discussion. It was not what I said-it was my willingness to listen fully.

Avoiding Miscommunication

Sometimes words get said in a rush and bring about misunderstandings or conflict. Pausing to take a deep breath before answering may bring about clarity and reduce friction.

Creating Meaningful Connections

Pausing allows space for authentic engagement. In silent moments, one can feel the emotions, intent, and the unspoken word, and so a bond may be developed much deeper.

Cultivating Silence and Pause in Daily Life

Practice the art of silence and pause and try to incorporate it into your life; it does not require Herculean efforts, but smaller, deliberate ones. Start with sitting in silence for a few minutes a day with no distractions or diversions at all, just breathe. Try small pauses in your day: pause before sending an email response, a break between tasks, or even during a conversation to reflect and renew. Even a little walk without your earbuds can bring a pretty deep, reassuring clarity. Over time, these simple practices accumulate, reduce stress, enhance concentration, and create deeper self-awareness. Consistency builds up these moments of calm to deeply change how one responds to life's demands.

Mindfulness and Meditation

Meditation is probably one of the best ways of cultivating silence: whether it's focusing on the breath for some minutes or just doing a guided meditation, such moments of stillness can completely transform your day.

Taking breaks and practicing self-care

Take a break, whether you step out of your desk, take a walk, or have a quiet cup of tea. This will give you time to recharge and come back with renewed focus.

Creating a Calm Ambiance

Your environment also plays a role in creating silence. Often, having a quiet place in your home, or adding plants, or soft lighting in your home, would make much of the difference.

Overcoming Challenges and Resistance

Accepting silence and pause is not an easy thing to do, especially today when there's a world around us that screams activity and connection as a badge of productivity. It's difficult to sit still because, by sitting still, one might recall and feel uncomfortable emotions or thoughts one has been trying to avoid. Our minds, wired to be always stimulated, could rebel against this quietness and fill the gap with worry or restlessness. However, such discomfort is an entrance to growth. Gently leaning into the silence teaches a person to listen to himself and find hidden truths and clarity, a practice not easy at first but deeply rewarding in the long run.

Common Obstacles

Fear of silence is real. There are so many people who have a fear of silence because, for one thing, they will be compelled to face their thoughts. Moreover, distractions, self-doubts, and the perpetual pull of technology make it a challenge to build silence.

Steps to Overcome Resistance

Start with little changes. Start with a few minutes of silence per day and work up from there. Techniques such as journaling or guided meditations can ease the process. Don't get frustrated with yourself. Silence, like any other skill, takes time to learn.

A Life Transformed by Silence and Pause

The more I leaned into silence and pause, the more I saw its ripples. It brings me peace, clarity, and connection—connection not just with others but also with myself. Challenges in life become less intimidating, and the joyous moments are more colorful. One evening, after such a frantic day, I went outside and sat in silence. Everything else just seemed to slow down—the rustling of leaves, the buzzing of life even from afar, and the quiet rhythm of my breathing. At that moment, I knew the sensation of belonging-the universe reminding one of its expanse and even one's place in it.

Conclusion: Embracing the Power of Silence and Pause

We so often take the gifts of silence and pause for granted, though they hold great transformative power. In a world that constantly calls out for attention, these moments provide a safe haven, teaching us to listen not superficially but deeply. They invite us to tune into ourselves, really listen to others, and be awake to the cadences of our world. Sometimes, we simply need to let go of hurrying, acting, and trying to fill the space in any given moment because the deepest, most meaningful moments are born simply from being there.

Imagine the difference between a cacophonous, frenetic day marked by constant interruptions and noise compared to a space that gives permission for thoughtful pause. It isn't just calm; it invites you to challenges, considered decision making, and delighting in tiny beauty often drowned in the whirl.

Incorporating silence and pause do not require much change. Simply start small, take a quiet moment between tasks to reset the mind, and pause in the middle of conversation to gather one's thoughts before responding. Spend time in nature, allowing the peace it instills in the world to infuse into you. Such mundane activities can nudge you towards more peaceful living, greater self-awareness, and more genuine relationships.

In the end, life is not about what we do, but about how well we experience it. Silence and pause remind us to cherish those ephemeral moments that make life worth living. They remind us that meaningful life is not having to be always busy but to find a fun, meaningful depth and purpose in every step of the journey. Let them accompany you with silence and allow them to guide you to a fulfilling and well-centered existence.

YOUR THOUGHTS

CHAPTER 9

(THE POWER OF MANIFESTATION)

Introduction to Manifestation 101

Manifestation isn't some magical art that belongs to the realm of the pious or something whimsical from a daydream world, lost in fantasy and unrelated to reality. It is a powerful, tangible process, based on the intentional adjustment of your thoughts, emotions, and actions towards bringing your wishes into being. In its essence, manifestation revolves around clarity, focus, and intention: to know what one wants with an exactness, and to energize it towards it.

It's like a seed in fertile ground. The intent is the seed, and then your concentrated thinking and positive emotion are the sunshine and water, and it is the careful tending that leads to its eventual growth. So, manifestation has nothing to do with wishy-washiness; it actually requires a beautiful interplay between mindset and work, with belief in the limitless capacity of the universe to help us out.

This process requires some trust. Trust in self, ability, and the unseen forces working for you. Anytime you align your internal energy with action on the outside, you create an enormous force that attracts what you want be it people, circumstances, or opportunities. It attracts all that resonate with your desires. Manifestation is more than a technique or an approach to achieve goals-it is a conscious way of creating a life full of purpose, joy, and fulfillment.

Consider a young artist Ari, with a dream of hosting her solitary art exhibit. She didn't stop at simply dreaming; Maya painted relentlessly with visions of what it would one day be like, with her arts adorning those gallery walls to share with like-minded people. These stories show and demonstrate the manifestations of change when manifesting with intent, emotion, and purpose behind them.

Understanding the Law of Attraction

Manifestation works on the base principle of Law of Attraction, where it is said that like attracts like. According to this universal law, whatever a person thinks and feels has its own energy vibration and acts as an attractor of the universe, attracting energies of similar frequency into your world. Your internal world manifests itself in your outer world.

Imagine your mind like a powerful broadcasting station, transmitting signals into the universe every second. All thoughts, either positive or negative, have different energies. The more emotion a thought is bound to—such as joy, fear, or doubt—the higher its frequency gets. For instance, if you envision an exciting career with confidence, then you enhance the chances of bringing opportunities that resonate with that vision. But if you imagine success but feel insecurities and fear of being an inadequate person, then these opposing signals tend to weaken your manifesting power by causing you to be confused.

Clear intention and alignment must be present in order to manifest effectively. One must not merely want something, but the thoughts, emotions, and beliefs all need to be in resonance with that wanting. Combining a clear vision with belief and positive emotion creates a centered energy field, which is heard by the universe. Alignment can be like a magnet that pulls in the right people, opportunities, and circumstances toward supporting your goal.

The Law of Attraction is not like wishful thinking; it's more about intentional living. When you acknowledge what you are thinking and feeling, you are able to focus your energy in the direction you want your life to go by being aware of your thoughts and emotions. This world is bountiful and constantly responds through different frequencies compared to yours. When you give off positivity, confidence, and belief, then experiences will align to mirror these energies, demonstrating that the ability to manifest dreams lies in aligning the mind, heart, and spirit.

Preparing for Manifestation

You must have a firm foundation before manifesting your dreams:

Setting Clear Intentions

Vague wishes lead to vague results. Talking about, "I want to be successful" is vague. Instead, go specific: "I want a promotion in my field by the end of next year." That is how the dream turns into an actionable goal.

Letting go of limiting beliefs

Limiting beliefs are silent saboteurs. For example, thinking "I am not good enough" or "I don't deserve this" will hinder the manifestation process. Rewrite your inner script. Use "I can and will" instead of "I can't." Be afraid, but not of what people might think or say about your reality. Do not let them dictate your reality.

Cultivate a positive mindset

A fertile mind is where manifestation thrives. One must practice gratitude on a daily basis, affirmations, and journaling to wire their subconscious into seeing the good in everything. See yourself not just to the destination but the process, too, in optimism and happiness.

Visualization Techniques for Manifestation

Visualization is a power tool that combines your subconscious mind with conscious reality.

The Power of Visualization

As you vividly imagine your goal, you fire off the same neurons as if you were really going through the physical experience of having it. You essentially rewire your brain into thinking that this is possible.

Step-by-Step Visualization Guide

Go to a quiet, comfortable place with no distractions.

Clear your intent: Think of what you want to manifest.

With your eyes shut, imagine very vividly whatever you want in your life to happen. Think of all that you can possibly feel, touch, hear, and smell in the place, for example if you are to visualize a perfect house. You'd smell fresh paint, hear some laughter in the living room, and feel some warmth of sunshine coming through your windows.

Feel the feelings attached to reaching your dream. Feel excited, feel joyful, feel grateful.

Tips to Observe for Successful Visualization

Visualize daily at the same time.

Use vision boards or journaling to accompany mental imagery.

Use movement such as stretching or walking to maintain energy flow.

Emotions and Energy in Manifestation

The emotional state is what gives manifestation fuel.

The Role of Emotions

Happy, grateful, and loving emotions tend to expand the field of energy and can make it easier to attract what one wants. Emotions of anger or fear can give rise to resistance.

Managing Negative Emotions

Life is bound to bring its share of challenges. Rather than suppressing negative emotions, let them out and release them. Journaling, meditation, or talking to a trusted friend or family member can help clear emotional blockages.

Energy and Vibration

Everything in the universe vibrates at a specific frequency. Putting yourself in alignment with your intended outcome facilitates manifestation. Some of the simple techniques involved in raising one's vibrational energy are listening to positive songs, engaging in creative hobbies, or practicing mindfulness.

Taking Inspired Action

Manifestation is not passive. It calls for action.

The Importance of Action

Dreaming about achieving success without effort is similar to planting a seed without water; taking little or any step forward towards the dream signals to the universe that one is serious about it.

Listening to Intuition

Your intuition will point you in the direction of experiences that align with what you want in life. Tune into your gut feelings or coincidence, it could be the nudge from the universe.

Consistent and Focused Action

Manifestation is a journey and not a race. Break the goal into little doable steps and work consistently towards them. Be happy at the smallest progression. Celebrate every step forward, no matter how small.

Overcoming Obstacles and Trusting the Process

It requires patience and faith for manifestation to take place.

Common Obstacles

Self-doubts, fear of failure, impatience-the list of roadblocks goes on. Accept all these as part of the process and not as a failure indicator.

Trust the Process

The universe has mysterious ways and results may not be in line with your timing. Trust that detours or delays are on purpose, leading to something you may have wanted even less than what you were expecting.

Letting Go of Attachment

Attachment to the specific outcome causes resistance. Let go of your attachment to rigid expectations and instead focus on the essence of what you want—the feeling that this is going to bring—and let go of your expectation.

Maintaining a Manifestation Mindset

Manifestation is something that needs practice every day.

Gratitude and Appreciation

A feedback loop of abundance is the result of a grateful mind. Reflecting each day on your gratitude opens channels for more flow into your life.

Self-Care and Mindfulness

A rested, balanced mind is better able to sense opportunity. Cultivate practices that nurture body, mind, and spirit through yoga, a nature walk, or artistic activity.

Becoming a Manifestation Artist

Manifestation is the delicate dance of art and science, between seeing your dreams and taking grounded, purposeful action. It demands bold dreaming, expansive thinking, and unshakable belief in conjunction with a deep sense of being grounded in the present. It is the alignment of thought, feeling, and action with what you want to have in your life and trusting in the universe's timing to manifest that vision for you in the best possible way.

Becoming a manifestation artist is to embrace one's power as a creator. That the life one wants is not some far-fetched fantasy; it is an opportunity waiting to be brought into existence by one's intention, belief, and action. As you manifest every day, be open to the journey, even in the case of setbacks and challenges. They help you learn from them, thereby refining your vision and making your resolve stronger.

Success lies in balance; dream big but act deliberately, visualize your goals but ground them in actionable steps, trust the process but stay constant in your effort. The life you envision is not just hope or a wish but a reality waiting to unfurl.

The ability to manifest lives inside you, so believe in it, receive it, and apply it; your dreams come closer than ever to becoming part of your real life when the time is just right for that and you're ready as well to receive.

YOUR THOUGHTS

CHAPTER 10

(THE ART OF GRATITUDE)

"If we are grateful for what we have, then we will get more, and if we are not, then what we have will be taken away," - Rhonda Byrne

This quote is very profound in universality. Appreciation is more than a mere mannered response; it is an energized state affecting our reality. So, this quote fits well into what manifestation and Law of Attraction advocate, where all that matters for the transformation to take place, according to that power, is the recognition of gratitude within our lives.

Gratitude is like a magnet. More of what we appreciate tends to come our way. As we focus on the things we have and let there be authentic gratitude, it forms a vibration that is in harmony with abundance. This high-vibrational energy lets the universe know we're ready to accept more. Thus, being thankful for good health, quality relationships, or abundant opportunities automatically gets us in the right mind space to draw more blessings in our lives.

But if we are taking things for granted or are worried about what we do not have, then we work from a space of scarcity. Negative energy repels abundance and creates a vicious cycle of dissatisfaction. It's as if the universe reflects our inner state by taking away from us what we don't appreciate. We may fail to value the stable job or the loving relationship we had until it's too late and gone.

It's also a lesson in being mindful and in the moment. There are gifts we receive constantly throughout life—

little and large. Whether it is the air in our lungs, a meal prepared for us to eat, or the people surrounding us with support, noticing such gifts can lead to feeling more satisfied with one's existence. With the sense of gratitude to hold onto while undergoing troubles, the view changes for a person and his development potential and possibilities of happiness also open up.

Byrne's quote also reminds us that gratitude is an emotion that we need to imbibe in us. It's a practice. The more you are in flow with the universe, the more abundance, peace, and prosperity flow your way. And when we practice gratitude daily, we bring more and more into our lives of abundance, peace, and prosperity.

Imagine starting your day with a bland "*thank you*." It seems ordinary, even mechanical, as you accept gestures, or acknowledge being able to see another sunrise. But is this truly gratitude? If you ask me I would say gratitude is not just words; it is a very profound alignment of thought, emotion, and intention that transform ordinary things into something more extraordinary. It is a willingness to celebrate life's goodness with sincere appreciation and presence.

Real gratitude is a feeling born out of mindfulness. Let's say you go to the temple, you thank the lord for your health, but your mind is distracted - rushing through your prayers or cranky because there are so many people around. Similarly, whenever a house help serves you water, you mumble "thanks" without even looking at them. Although these actions are not necessarily without value, they just seem to lack that depth and emotional intensity that defines actual gratitude. Genuine gratitude is more than an automatic word, but rather one that is said with consciousness and full emotion.

Take a minute to think of how often we take the ordinary miracles in life for granted. The internet had become a lifeline during the pandemic. Online recipes became the family meal; streaming platforms became sources of comfort; children spent their days playing in online games. However, how many of us were ever thankful to the engineers, developers, and service providers who made this happen? Without whom all this is impossible?

Even something as basic as a meal involves an enormous amount of unseen efforts. The crops were grown by farmers, harvested and transported by workers, available in the shops by retailers, and prepared by someone before reaching our plates. But how many times when we sit to dine do we ever stop and remember to feel gratitude? Instead, our attention darts to phone screens or TV sets, claiming to "feel gratitude" without even feeling it.

That isn't to say we need to thank everyone who's brought a sense of well-being into our lives. What we need is the vibrational component of gratitude—the energy we tend out there in the universe. This energy turns on the Law of Attraction, the universal principle that reflects our inner state and gives us experiences corresponding to what we are focusing on.

If we write down all we have against what we do not have, then what we have would be limitless. However, we tend to focus on those very few things we do not have. That's lessening our vibration and creating a distance between what we're desiring and ourselves. Mostly, what happens is that either the timing is wrong or we're not in a state to receive those things.

Imagine ordering in the universe's cosmic kitchen. Once the order is placed, the universe starts gathering the ingredients to create the desired outcome. However, the dish will only arrive when the time is right, fitting your vibrations to your readiness. The orientation toward the question of "how" or "when" happens to just delay the process. Rather, detachment from those questions and having faith in the universe allows your desires to unfold as if effortlessly.

This principle of focus is easy enough, wherever your attention goes, energy follows, and that energy amplifies. If your focus is on self-doubt or how this manifestation business is going to play out, you are sending mixed messages. What works is trusting in the process, gratitude for all you already have, and staying at high vibrations.

Japanese scientist Dr. Masaru Emoto conducted a rather interesting experiment for this. He exposed water in three different containers to three various energies - love, gratitude, and hatred. Then, freezing the water and looking at it under a microscope, he compared the molecular structures. The results were unbelievable. Water to which hatred had been given would create chaotic and disjointed patterns, whereas love created harmonious pearl-like structures. But it was the water that was given gratitude that created the most beautiful crystalline patterns similar to diamonds.

This experiment makes one realize how much power words and emotions have on our surroundings and even ourselves. Considering the human body is made up of about 70% water, think of the ways your thoughts, words, and emotions impact your health and reality. Darkness and hate feed chaos; love and appreciation grow harmony and beauty.

Small things, like putting down complaints in place of appreciation or self-doubting with self-encouragement and routine acknowledgments with heartfelt thanks, are part of incorporating gratitude into daily life. Gratitude is a practice and a muscle that gets stronger the more it's used.

While waiting for a dream to materialize, gratitude helps stabilize the moment. Rather than dwelling on the end result, dwell on what is already given. This change keeps your vibration high and opens up the universe to adjust things in your favor. Gratitude, therefore, is a practice and a bridge between dreams and reality.

When you embrace gratitude, you will see how it transforms your mindset. You begin to see the world as abundant, rather than scarce. Your relationships grow deeper, because you're noticing and appreciating the people in your life. Opportunities become apparent, as like energy attracts you.

Gratitude is an art of noticing the extraordinary in ordinary things. One appreciates having a soft, comfortable bed; the convenience of technology; the efforts of people who have created, maintained, and delivered thousands of goods that make life so easy for everyone. The littlest blessings form a part of the interlacing threads that stitch together the very fabric of life.

Start small. Start your day listing three things you are thankful for. End it reflecting on moments that made you happy. Say it, write it, allowing the feeling of gratitude to sit deeply in. Gratitude isn't a state that's short-lived; it's a lifestyle that leads to fulfillment and abundance. Gratitude harmonizes with the rhythm of the universe. We see our lives as overflowing with blessings that just need to be recognized. What we receive changes not only because of gratitude but also in the way we view it. It is a journey that has become a dance through life, which leads us closer to our dreams.

When you open yourself to this art form, remember that the power to manifest is within you. The key to unlocking the treasures of life is gratitude. When you use it sincerely and in the present moment, miracles can occur and enhance your life in ways beyond imagination.

So, as we approach the end of this journey of transformation, it is time to reflect on the wisdom that has been shared throughout this book. We started with the foundation of manifestation and made sure to focus first on the power of clarity within your desires. Knowing what you really want and being precise with your intentions are the first steps to aligning oneself with the universe. From here, we discovered the Law of Attraction - how your mind and energy magnetize around you experiences that are in alignment with your inner state.

Gratitude turned out to be the foundation stone of manifestation. Appreciating what you already have raises your vibrational level, and the doors open to much more abundance. We learnt that the simple act of being thankful is enough to bring miracles when it is done from the heart.

Throughout the chapters, tools and techniques like visualization, affirmations, detachment, and inspired action were discussed. These are not just single moves but rather an integrated set of practices that move you toward your desired outcomes by trusting in the universe's timing.

Not only that but we have also discussed issues like how to overcome self-doubt, how to be resilient when there are delays, and how to trust the process. Manifestation in short requires patience, perseverance, and letting go of control.

Remember that manifestation is not a destination, but a lifelong journey as you close this book. Every thought, feeling, and action counts to create your reality. You are now holding the key to transforming your life with the principles outlined here, one aligned intention at a time. Believe, act, and receive; the universe will meet you halfway.

YOUR THOUGHTS

AUTHOR'S NOTE

My name is Priyanka Madan, and the one thing life has taught me if it has taught me anything at all is that the journey of life is never a straight line. It has never been a bed of roses for me, it was full of twists and turns, both of which has taught me a lot of things about myself as well as around me.

After attaining a graduation degree in economics, I plunged headlong into the corporate world. Like others at that age, I considered climbing up the professional ladder would be the road to fulfillment. In fact, to hone my skills further, I even did a diploma in Marketing and Public Relations. Everything seemed to be falling into place for a while, a great career that I was proud of and ticking all the right boxes left & right. What else could I possibly want?

But somehow, something didn't feel right. I felt that I was created for something greater, which was engraved in my spirit. It was not long before I realized what truly intrigued me - the human mind. I was naturally drawn to conversations which did not necessarily deal with the external but dwelled on so much more. From an innocent curiosity, it became an experience that changed everything for me, unlocking new thought patterns and a deeper understanding of people and their inner worlds. It made me realize that what people really needed wasn't advice or solutions;

they needed someone to genuinely listen to them. And I wanted to be that person in a world where people tend to rush by and create less space for other people to be heard.

I believe it was not chance but a gentle nudge in the right direction by the universe. That belief fueled my courage again to pivot—to a career with a deeper purpose of working close to people and their emotions and challenges and dreams.

Becoming a life coach felt like coming home to me. I am not a sage with all the answers; rather, I guide, support, and empower people to help them negotiate life's ups and downs. I bring not just my academic and professional experiences but also lessons from my own life to the table-the victories, failures, and all that is in between.

I often like to remind my clients and myself that life isn't perfect; it is all about the progress you make. It is about recognizing that every experience, good or bad, is a string in the tapestry of our existence. Every second contributes depth to our story, and each choice molds our path.

I am grateful to do what I do today. Be it helping a person find their clarity in some difficult decision-making process, helping someone regain his or her zest for life, or just listening when they want to talk about it, I do my job based on the fact that everybody deserves a purposeful and joyous life.

So, if you're reading this and wondering whether it's actually possible to take a step toward the life of your dreams, I want you to know: yes, you absolutely can, and I would feel honored to be walking along this journey with you.

ABOUT THE BOOK

The reason I wrote this book is extremely personal—the idea of it sprang from my own transformation. The information that fills the pages of this book is not some theory or concept; they are practices and principles that have had a dramatic influence on the way I choose to live and operate, increasing my standards, making my life more fulfilling. They have assisted me in shaping the life of my choice, and I'm certain that applying these methods can assist others to do the same.

This book is my attempt to share with you a roadmap—a guide toward manifesting the life you so desire. It is to make you understand that you're not just another person existing because, believe it or not, it took the whole universe to will this existence of yours. Imagine being the miscarried or aborted cell inside the womb. Think about that one cell, lost in oblivion, in some mother's uterus. Well, you managed to pass through it, and in itself, it's already evidence of the fact that you had a purpose to fulfill. Self-love should start with these thoughts.

Self-love is not just pampering and conditional self-esteem, but it's making your existence valuable, staying grounded, and being connected to your family and loved ones. It's loving yourself in such a way that does no harm to others, makes you live with harmony, and lets you understand your role in the bigger tapestry of life.

Life, as far as I have seen, flows like a river. Much of its course has been predetermined; however, there are portions we can still do something about. Water follows naturally in its own path, but you can dig an alternate course for it if you want it to flow in another direction. It is the same with people or circumstances in one's life-we cannot choose many of them, but we do have a choice as to how to deal with each and what each moment means to us.

The key lies within our thoughts; they are actually the architects of our reality. If you are to change your life around, you'll have to think differently first. When we deny life's flowing current, life becomes a difficult swim. If we learn how to go along with its normal flow, the flow of life becomes smoother and more fulfilling; it gets filled with greater peace. It is important to realize that the essence of harmony revolves around acceptance instead of expectation.

This book represents my raw, unfiltered journey—my thoughts, struggles, and breakthroughs. It's a call to all readers to explore their own paths, discover their own purpose in life, and live a life they actually love. Understanding the interaction of karmic lessons with dharmic choices can better align us to the universe's plan while taking empowered decisions in our lives.

This is not just my story alone; It is everyone's truth. We are characters in a far greater play and are pieces of the masterpiece of the universe. Each of us has their own role, and it is for us to play that role with purpose, grace, and authenticity.

Let life flow, and you will find it leads you exactly where you are meant to be.

GRATITUDE JOURNAL

Journal is owned by

Name:

Dedicated to:

(Name of your God or Person)

My Intention:

(Your plan or purpose)

Starting Date:

"When I started counting blessings, my whole life turned around." – Willie Nelson

WHAT IS A JOURNAL?

A personal space.

Record thoughts, feelings and experiences.

Reflect on our life and growth.

Learn from our experiences.

Cultivate self-awareness and introspection.

Optimistic life.

Clarity of thoughts.

High vibration and high energy.

Feeling of contentment.

Learn to celebrate success.

Focus on goodness in life.

Better Relationships.

We get aware of our actions and intentions.

Transferring our energy onto a paper to be an observer of our thoughts.

Help you explore who you are and where you can be.

"Gratitude is a muscle, more we practice,

better we get in Life."

WHAT TO WRITE IN JOURNAL

Journal is like our photo album. As the year passes by album reveals physical changes in a person whereas journal reflects your mental changes.

Filling a journal is like having a conversation with yourself. It will help you analyse past behaviour and take corrective actions. Journal is your autobiography.

- Journal should capture your observations and experiences.

- You can capture your mistakes and describe emotional responses to life's experiences. Capture joys and sorrows. All emotions are the effects of some cause. The more deeply you dive into the event, the better the understanding you will have, which will lead to better decision making.

- Capture and create new ideas.

- Record financial ideas.

- Mention relationship ideas.

- Write health related ideas.

- Create a system of your own.

"Maintaining a journal be conscious of using your mind as a thinking factory rather than a filing cabinet."

Date_____

Today I feel:

_____
_____
_____
_____

Today I have learnt:

_____
_____
_____
_____

Today I'm proud of:

_____
_____
_____
_____

Today I commit to improve:

_____
_____
_____
_____

Important things to do tomorrow

_____
_____
_____
_____

Date_____

Today I feel:

_____
_____
_____
_____

Today I have learnt:

_____
_____
_____
_____

Today I'm proud of:

_____
_____
_____
_____

Today I commit to improve:

_____
_____
_____
_____

Important things to do tomorrow

_____
_____
_____
_____

Date_____

Today I feel:

_____
_____
_____
_____

Today I have learnt:

_____
_____
_____
_____

Today I'm proud of:

_____
_____
_____
_____

Today I commit to improve:

_____
_____
_____
_____

Important things to do tomorrow

_____
_____
_____
_____

Date_____

Today I feel:

_____
_____
_____
_____

Today I have learnt:

_____
_____
_____
_____

Today I'm proud of:

_____
_____
_____
_____

Today I commit to improve:

_____
_____
_____
_____

Important things to do tomorrow

_____
_____
_____
_____

Date_____

Today I feel:

_____
_____
_____
_____

Today I have learnt:

_____
_____
_____
_____

Today I'm proud of:

_____
_____
_____
_____

Today I commit to improve:

_____
_____
_____
_____

Important things to do tomorrow

_____
_____
_____
_____

Date_____

Today I feel:

_____
_____
_____
_____

Today I have learnt:

_____
_____
_____
_____

Today I'm proud of:

_____
_____
_____
_____

Today I commit to improve:

_____
_____
_____
_____

Important things to do tomorrow

_____
_____
_____
_____

Date_____

Today I feel:

_____
_____
_____
_____

Today I have learnt:

_____
_____
_____
_____

Today I'm proud of:

_____
_____
_____
_____

Today I commit to improve:

_____
_____
_____
_____

Important things to do tomorrow

_____
_____
_____
_____

Date_____

Today I feel:

_____
_____
_____
_____

Today I have learnt:

_____
_____
_____
_____

Today I'm proud of:

_____
_____
_____
_____

Today I commit to improve:

_____
_____
_____
_____

Important things to do tomorrow

_____
_____
_____
_____

Date_____

Today I feel:

_____
_____
_____
_____

Today I have learnt:

_____
_____
_____
_____

Today I'm proud of:

_____
_____
_____
_____

Today I commit to improve:

_____
_____
_____
_____

Important things to do tomorrow

_____
_____
_____
_____

Date_____

Today I feel:

_____
_____
_____
_____

Today I have learnt:

_____
_____
_____
_____

Today I'm proud of:

_____
_____
_____
_____

Today I commit to improve:

_____
_____
_____
_____

Important things to do tomorrow

_____
_____
_____
_____

Date_____

Today I feel:

_____
_____
_____
_____

Today I have learnt:

_____
_____
_____
_____

Today I'm proud of:

_____
_____
_____
_____

Today I commit to improve:

_____
_____
_____
_____

Important things to do tomorrow

_____
_____
_____
_____

Date_____

Today I feel:

_____
_____
_____
_____

Today I have learnt:

_____
_____
_____
_____

Today I'm proud of:

_____
_____
_____
_____

Today I commit to improve:

_____
_____
_____
_____

Important things to do tomorrow

_____
_____
_____
_____

Date_____

Today I feel:

_____
_____
_____
_____

Today I have learnt:

_____
_____
_____
_____

Today I'm proud of:

_____
_____
_____
_____

Today I commit to improve:

_____
_____
_____
_____

Important things to do tomorrow

_____
_____
_____
_____

Date_____

Today I feel:

_____
_____
_____
_____

Today I have learnt:

_____
_____
_____
_____

Today I'm proud of:

_____
_____
_____
_____

Today I commit to improve:

_____
_____
_____
_____

Important things to do tomorrow

_____
_____
_____
_____

Date_____

Today I feel:

_____
_____
_____
_____

Today I have learnt:

_____
_____
_____
_____

Today I'm proud of:

_____
_____
_____
_____

Today I commit to improve:

_____
_____
_____
_____

Important things to do tomorrow

_____
_____
_____
_____

Date_____

Today I feel:

_____
_____
_____
_____

Today I have learnt:

_____
_____
_____
_____

Today I'm proud of:

_____
_____
_____
_____

Today I commit to improve:

_____
_____
_____
_____

Important things to do tomorrow

_____
_____
_____
_____

Date_____

Today I feel:

_____

_____

_____

Today I have learnt:

_____

_____

_____

Today I'm proud of:

_____

_____

_____

Today I commit to improve:

_____

_____

_____

Important things to do tomorrow

_____
_____
_____
_____

Date_____

Today I feel:

_____
_____
_____
_____

Today I have learnt:

_____
_____
_____
_____

Today I'm proud of:

_____
_____
_____
_____

Today I commit to improve:

_____
_____
_____
_____

Important things to do tomorrow
___

Date_____

Today I feel:

_____
_____
_____
_____

Today I have learnt:

_____
_____
_____
_____

Today I'm proud of:

_____
_____
_____
_____

Today I commit to improve:

_____
_____
_____
_____

Important things to do tomorrow

_____
_____
_____
_____

Date_____

Today I feel:

_____
_____
_____
_____

Today I have learnt:

_____
_____
_____
_____

Today I'm proud of:

_____
_____
_____
_____

Today I commit to improve:

_____
_____
_____
_____

Important things to do tomorrow

_____
_____
_____
_____

Date_____

Today I feel:

_____
_____
_____
_____

Today I have learnt:

_____
_____
_____
_____

Today I'm proud of:

_____
_____
_____
_____

Today I commit to improve:

_____
_____
_____
_____

Important things to do tomorrow

_____
_____
_____
_____

Date_____

Today I feel:

_____
_____
_____
_____

Today I have learnt:

_____
_____
_____
_____

Today I'm proud of:

_____
_____
_____
_____

Today I commit to improve:

_____
_____
_____
_____

Important things to do tomorrow

_____
_____
_____
_____

Date_____

Today I feel:

_____
_____
_____
_____

Today I have learnt:

_____
_____
_____
_____

Today I'm proud of:

_____
_____
_____
_____

Today I commit to improve:

_____
_____
_____
_____

Important things to do tomorrow

_____
_____
_____
_____

Date_____

Today I feel:

_____
_____
_____
_____

Today I have learnt:

_____
_____
_____
_____

Today I'm proud of:

_____
_____
_____
_____

Today I commit to improve:

_____
_____
_____
_____

Important things to do tomorrow

_____
_____
_____
_____

Date_____

Today I feel:

_____
_____
_____
_____

Today I have learnt:

_____
_____
_____
_____

Today I'm proud of:

_____
_____
_____
_____

Today I commit to improve:

_____
_____
_____
_____

Important things to do tomorrow

_____
_____
_____
_____

Date_____

Today I feel:

_____
_____
_____
_____

Today I have learnt:

_____
_____
_____
_____

Today I'm proud of:

_____
_____
_____
_____

Today I commit to improve:

_____
_____
_____
_____

Important things to do tomorrow

_____
_____
_____
_____

Date_____

Today I feel:

_____
_____
_____
_____

Today I have learnt:

_____
_____
_____
_____

Today I'm proud of:

_____
_____
_____
_____

Today I commit to improve:

_____
_____
_____
_____

Important things to do tomorrow

_____
_____
_____
_____

Date_____

Today I feel:

_____
_____
_____
_____

Today I have learnt:

_____
_____
_____
_____

Today I'm proud of:

_____
_____
_____
_____

Today I commit to improve:

_____
_____
_____
_____

Important things to do tomorrow

_____
_____
_____
_____

Date_____

Today I feel:

_____
_____
_____
_____

Today I have learnt:

_____
_____
_____
_____

Today I'm proud of:

_____
_____
_____
_____

Today I commit to improve:

_____
_____
_____
_____

Important things to do tomorrow

_____
_____
_____
_____

Date_____

Today I feel:

_____
_____
_____
_____

Today I have learnt:

_____
_____
_____
_____

Today I'm proud of:

_____
_____
_____
_____

Today I commit to improve:

_____
_____
_____
_____

Important things to do tomorrow

_____
_____
_____
_____

www.ingramcontent.com/pod-product-compliance
Lightning Source LLC
LaVergne TN
LVHW041706070526
838199LV00045B/1226